# EMBRACING THE FUTURE OF WORK

*15 Actionable Strategies for Inclusive, High-Performing Organizations*

LUASKYA C. NONON, Esq.

Copyright © 2025 by Luaskya C. Nonon, Esq., Equity Principle Consulting, LLC

All rights reserved.

No part of this book may be copied, reproduced, stored in a retrieval system, or transmitted in any form or by any means—electronic, mechanical, photocopying, recording, or otherwise—without the prior written permission of the publisher, except for brief quotations in critical reviews or articles, which must include full attribution to the author, book title, and publication year.

Published by Equity Principle Consulting, LLC

**ISBN (Print): 979-8-9925324-0-1**
**ISBN (eBook): 979-8-9925324-1-8**
**Library of Congress Control Number: 2025901828**

This book is a work of nonfiction. Any references to real people, organizations, or events are intended solely for illustrative or educational purposes. The opinions expressed are those of the author and do not necessarily reflect the views of any organization with which they are affiliated.

**Disclaimer:**

*The information in this book is provided for general informational purposes only. The author and publisher make no representations or warranties regarding its applicability to any specific situation.*

**Printed in the United States of America.**

## Dedication

*To my family and friends, thank you for
your continued love and support!*

*Special shout out to Justice, Jaxen and Johnny,
for being my biggest cheerleaders!*

# Contents

Preface .................................................................................................. 1

Introduction ......................................................................................... 6

## Chapter 1: Embedding DE&I in Your Organizational Strategy: A Blueprint for Lasting Change ........................................................... 12

Actionable Strategy #1: Integrate DE&I into Core Business Strategies ....... 23

Actionable Strategy #2: Leverage Data for DE&I Success ......................... 29

Actionable Strategy #3: Track and Measure DE&I Progress ..................... 35

## Chapter 2: Harnessing Technology and AI for Inclusivity ........... 46

Actionable Strategy #4: Implement Ethical AI Practices ........................... 53

Actionable Strategy #5: Leverage Technology to Achieve Inclusivity for All Employees .................................................................................. 63

## Chapter 3: Building Inclusive Leadership Pipeline for the Future .................................................................................................... 72

Actionable Strategy #6: Invest in Inclusive Leadership Training ............... 79

Actionable Strategy #7: Create Career Pathways through Mentorship and Sponsorship .................................................................................. 85

## Chapter 4: Adapting to a Dynamic Workforce ............................. 92

Actionable Strategy #8: Cultivate Inclusivity in Remote and Hybrid Teams 99

Actionable Strategy #9: Adopt Flexible Work Arrangements: A Key to Engagement ................................................................................. 105

## Chapter 5: Fostering Employee Well-being and Resilience ......... 114

Actionable Strategy #10: Link Mental Health and DE&I for Holistic Support ................................................................................................... 119

Actionable Strategy #11: Cultivate a Culture of Psychological Safety to Drive Innovation ........................................................................................... 125

Actionable Strategy #12: Engage Employees Through Listening Sessions 133

# Chapter 6: Navigating DE&I Challenges in Today's Polarized Climate .................................................................................................. 142

Actionable Strategy #13: Resist Anti-DE&I Pressure ................................. 149

Actionable Strategy #14: Reject Institutional Neutrality ........................... 155

Actionable Strategy #15: Champion Equity ................................................ 161

# Conclusion: Leading the Future of Work with Purpose and Values ........................................................................................................... 170

Case Studies ...................................................................................... 174

Epilogue ............................................................................................. 180

About The Author ............................................................................. 186

# Preface

As a second-year law student at the University of North Carolina School of Law, I sat in my Constitutional Law class feeling deeply unsettled. Reading the Constitution and learning about the historical context surrounding its drafting, I was reminded that these founding documents were not written with people who look like me in mind. The laws, as originally crafted, were never intended to extend rights, privileges, and justice to Black people like me. While subsequent amendments have broadened their applicability to include all men and women, exclusions persist in their application, interpretation, and enforcement to this day.

I am a first-generation Afro-Latina woman from Brooklyn, New York. Growing up, I understood that my life, liberty, and pursuit of happiness would not be as zealously protected as others'. Yet, here I am—the first in my family to become an attorney, consultant, and author. I built a career as an employment law and corporate transactions attorney and have since evolved into an award-winning diversity leader, equity strategist, consultant, and speaker.

My career has been defined by disrupting systems, challenging inequities, and helping others do the same. As of this writing, I stand among the 5% of lawyers in the United States who are Black and the 6% who are Hispanic. I was born to disrupt the status quo, and I have every intention of continuing to do just that.

Laws governing workplace culture and employee treatment are grounded in anti-discrimination principles. These laws exist to protect employees from harm and prevent discriminatory practices—but they do not create structures that allow historically disenfranchised employees to thrive. They don't offer guidance on how to build workplaces where employees flourish. Compliance with the law ensures employees survive the workplace, but it does not ensure they thrive in it.

As long as you aren't discriminating against employees or fostering a hostile work environment, you're likely on solid legal ground. But here's the truth: compliance alone is not enough to become a company prepared for the future of work, where the nature of work, the workforce, and the workplace itself are expected to evolve in unprecedented ways.

A compliance-based culture may enable companies to check boxes, meet regulatory requirements, and avoid legal trouble. It may even allow them to market and sell products, satisfy customers, and generate profits. But it will not enable them to lead in innovation, capture significant market share, or become the type of organization that thrives in the future of work. Companies that aspire to build inclusive, people-first cultures cannot rely on compliance alone. They must go beyond the minimum.

This book is for corporate leaders who are ready to go beyond compliance and make a lasting impact—those committed to building people-first cultures but unsure how to create workplaces that are truly equitable and inclusive. If that sounds like you, this book was written with you in mind.

*Embracing the Future of Work: 15 Actionable Strategies for Inclusive, High-Performing Organizations* is more than a guide—it's a call to action. It challenges you to lead with equity, to foster workplace cultures where everyone has the opportunity to thrive, and to champion the principles of inclusion and innovation.

Together, we can shape a future where workplaces truly work for everyone—driving innovation, enhancing profitability, and cultivating a culture of equity, inclusion, and high performance.

# Introduction

> *"It is not the strongest of the species that survive, nor the most intelligent, but the one most responsive to change."*
>
> — ***Charles Darwin***

This book operates on the premise that becoming a company capable of meeting the evolving demands of today's ever-changing workforce requires leveraging the principles and strategies of diversity, equity, and inclusion (DE&I). If you're reading this, you're likely either curious about these principles or seeking to understand how DE&I strategies can serve as an effective response to these workforce demands. In either case, it's important that we establish a shared foundation—clarifying the terminology used throughout this book and its relevance to building sustainable, inclusive workplaces.

## What Is It?

Diversity, Equity, and Inclusion (DE&I) is a strategic framework for acknowledging and addressing the disparities within laws, institutions, systems, and policies that perpetuate the subjugation of certain groups over others. These disparities act as roadblocks, impeding the advancement and progress of marginalized communities, making it increasingly difficult for them to thrive in various spaces, including the workplace.

## Why Is It Important?

DE&I has evolved from initiatives like the Civil Rights Movement and Affirmative Action, which were initially focused on extending privileges and rights historically denied to Black Americans. While those efforts primarily addressed racial injustice, DE&I is broader, encompassing the full spectrum of human identity- including gender, sexual orientation, socioeconomic status, disability, and more.

DE&I strategies aim to dismantle these roadblocks by embedding fairness and inclusion into the systems we operate within—whether that's in business, education, or healthcare. When workplaces commit to DE&I, they cultivate an environment where everyone's contributions are recognized, valued, and leveraged for the organization's collective success.

In the workplace, DE&I aims to implement sustainable strategies that increase diverse representation, embed fairness and equity principles, and create environments where all employees can thrive. The goal is to enhance the workplace experience so that it is welcoming, inclusive, and respectful of everyone's identity. A 2018 Deloitte report indicated that organizations with inclusive cultures are twice as likely to exceed financial goals, three times as likely to be high-performing, six times more likely to be innovative and agile and eight times more likely to achieve better business. [1]

## Why Now?

While DE&I efforts have been around for decades, its prominence surged during the social reckoning of the summer of 2020. The convergence of several events—global protests against racial injustice, political polarization, and the COVID-19 pandemic—highlighted the systemic inequalities embedded within our society and workplaces.

---

[1] Bourke, J., & Dillon, B. (2018). The diversity and inclusion revolution: Eight powerful truths. Deloitte Review, (22). Retrieved from https://www2.deloitte.com/content/dam/insights/us/articles/4209_Diversity-and-inclusion-revolution/DI_Diversity-and-inclusion-revolution.pdf

The COVID-19 pandemic gave many the opportunity to reflect on the quality of life and reconsider how work fits into their broader aspirations. Living with the fear of contracting a deadly virus and experiencing personal loss shifted societal priorities. This shift has permanently altered the social contract between employers and employees, rendering pre-pandemic norms obsolete.

Today's employees expect more than just safe, harassment-free workplaces—they seek work-life balance, alignment with their employer's values, environments that honor their full identities, and meaningful opportunities for growth.

For businesses, the question is no longer whether to engage in DE&I (even though there is a lot of noise to do contrary…we'll address this in Chapter 6), it's how to embed DE&I principles into every layer of your organization to meet the evolving expectations of employees and customers.

Leaders who adapt will position their companies for long-term success, while those who resist will struggle to remain relevant in an increasingly inclusive marketplace.

## What This Book Offers

*Embracing the Future of Work: 15 Actionable Strategies for Inclusive, High-Performing Organizations* provides corporate leaders with practical tools to navigate the evolving demands of today's workforce. Through actionable strategies, reflective exercises, and strategic guidance, this book equips you to build a workplace culture that is inclusive, adaptable, and positioned for sustained success.

Embedding DE&I principles into your corporate framework isn't just about meeting employee expectations—it's about future-proofing your organization. This book challenges you to rethink how you lead, how your employees engage, and the environment you create to help them thrive.

## The Stakes

Research[2] shows that companies committed to DE&I principles outperform competitors and capture greater market share. Conversely, companies that resist adapting to evolving workforce expectations and marketplace demands will struggle. They will face challenges in attracting top talent, fail to innovate, and risk losing their competitive edge—ultimately setting themselves on a path to decline.

But it doesn't have to be that way. You can embrace the call from both employees and customers to lead with intention, align your strategies with DE&I principles, and shape the future of work for your company.

Let's get started.

---

[2] The Cigna Group. (n.d.). *10 stats that show why diversity, equity, and inclusion are good for business*. Retrieved December 21, 2024, from https://newsroom.thecignagroup.com/10-stats-diversity-equity-inclusion-good-for-business

# Chapter 1:
# Embedding DE&I in Your Organizational Strategy: A Blueprint for Lasting Change

*"The best way to predict the future is to create it."*

— ***Peter Drucker***

To remain competitive in a rapidly evolving marketplace, forward-thinking leaders understand that aligning equity and inclusion principles with business strategies is essential. Embedding DE&I strategies into the fabric of an organization shapes its workplace culture in ways that meet the changing expectations of today's workforce while driving business growth and long-term success.

## Start with Purpose and Values

Developing a strategic DE&I plan begins with revisiting your company's purpose and core values. Ask yourself:

- **What are our company's core values and purpose?**
- **Are these values rooted in people-first principles?**
- **Do they align with our goals to advance equity and inclusion?**

These are not questions for your DE&I team to answer in isolation. Your executive team and other key stakeholders must be actively involved in this conversation. The goal is to understand who you are as a company and how that identity informs your approach to advancing equity and inclusion within your organization.

Once this alignment is clear, you can move forward with crafting a plan that integrates DE&I principles into your broader business strategy. Keep in mind that advancing DE&I is a long-term commitment—a marathon, not a sprint. While hiring external consultants can be beneficial, your internal DE&I team should also have a leading voice in shaping this strategy.

# A Strategic Approach Inspired by Product Life-Cycle Management

Having spent my career supporting information technology companies, I became familiar with the product development cycle. Surprisingly, I found striking similarities between the product development and lifecycle management process and the DE&I strategic planning process. In product development, the stages typically include:

1. Ideation
2. Product Development
3. Testing
4. Product Launch
5. Continuous Improvement

When applied to DE&I strategic planning, these same stages provide a roadmap for success.

## 1. Ideation: Build a Vision for Change

Once you've evaluated your core values and assessed where your organization currently stands, the next step is ideation—brainstorming actionable ways to build a more inclusive and equitable workplace.

Leaders who excel in this phase rely on employee data to identify potential interventions that address the unique needs of their workforce. For example, employee feedback may reveal concerns related to psychological safety, limited career advancement opportunities, or inadequate access to development resources. These insights inform the design of DE&I interventions tailored to address employee concerns.

Just as in product development, leaders must also anticipate potential challenges or resistance to certain initiatives during this stage. This foresight helps organizations avoid future missteps and ensures the ideation process is both innovative and practical.

## 2. Product Development: Design Your Interventions

Once ideas are generated, the next step is to design DE&I interventions. This stage requires thoughtful planning to ensure interventions are aligned with the company's purpose, business objectives, and the expressed needs of employees. It is during this phase that leaders shift from broad concepts to concrete, actionable initiatives that can be successfully implemented.

Effective intervention design prioritizes clarity, alignment, and responsiveness. Clarity ensures that employees and leaders alike understand the "what" and "why" behind the initiative. Alignment guarantees that interventions are directly connected to the company's overarching goals, values, and DE&I aspirations. Responsiveness ensures the design addresses the specific needs raised by employees or revealed through workforce analysis.

The development phase is where strategy becomes action. Companies must carefully consider how to structure their initiatives to ensure they are practical, relevant, and feasible within the organization's current environment. It is during this phase that the team may discover further research is warranted to determine the appropriate intervention. For example, a review of your people policies and programs may need to be conducted to determine what improvements need to be made.

While there may be a temptation to rush toward implementation, taking the time to properly design interventions increase the likelihood of success. Rushed initiatives are more likely to fail, leading to frustration, wasted resources, and employee distrust in the process.

When designing DE&I interventions, it's essential to ask:

- **Does this initiative align with our company's mission, vision, and purpose?**
- **How does this intervention support our business objectives?**
- **Is this intervention responsive to the needs and feedback of our employees?**
- **What potential barriers to success exist, and how will we address them?**

DE&I interventions should be tailored and specific rather than generic, one-size-fits-all solutions. Consider how an initiative will be perceived by different employee groups and whether it creates equitable access to opportunities for all. For example, an initiative to increase access to professional development may not be as effective if employees with caregiving responsibilities can't attend training during business hours. In such cases, offering on-demand, self-paced learning opportunities might be a more inclusive approach.

The development phase is also an opportunity to engage employees and key stakeholders. Employees closest to the work are often best positioned to offer insights on what is needed to create a more inclusive experience. Their voices should be included in the design process. Leaders should consult employee resource groups (ERGs), people managers, and representatives from various departments to gather input. Not only does this increase buy-in, but it also surfaces critical vulnerabilities that senior leaders or DE&I teams may not have recognized.

The goal is not speed—it's sustainability and impact. By taking the time to design thoughtful, intentional interventions, companies increase the likelihood of success, avoid costly missteps, and build a more inclusive, people-first workplace culture. A well-developed initiative is one that:

- Has a clear purpose and connection to larger company goals.
- Addresses a specific employee or business need.
- Is tested and adjusted based on employee feedback before launch.

Designing with intention and precision ensures the impact of your DE&I interventions will be lasting and meaningful.

## 3. Testing: Pilot Before You Launch

Here's where most organizations falter. Many jump straight from development to implementation without testing their initiatives first. But in product development, no company would dream of launching a new product without first running prototypes through multiple tests. The same logic applies to DE&I initiatives.

One effective strategy is to pilot DE&I initiatives within specific departments or divisions before rolling them out company-wide. For instance, if you're launching a mentorship program, begin with one department or region, track the results, and use those insights to refine the approach before a broader rollout. This phased approach minimizes risk, increases employee engagement, and provides leaders with an opportunity to test, learn, and adapt their strategies before a full-scale implementation. It's a more cautious but far more effective strategy than rolling out initiatives broadly and hoping for success.

## 4. Product Launch: Full Deployment

Once the testing phase is complete and you've identified interventions that yield positive results, it's time to roll them out across the broader organization. The next stage mirrors a product launch. Leaders should focus on clear communication to the workforce, highlighting the rationale for the intervention, how it will benefit employees, and what success will look like. Then there's the final stage in the process.

## 5. Continuous Improvement: Monitoring and Adapting for Sustained Success

In product lifecycle management, the continuous improvement phase focuses on monitoring the product's performance, deploying minor updates to address defects, and implementing major enhancements to improve functionality and user experience. Similarly, in DE&I strategic plan implementation, this phase is crucial for ensuring long-term impact and relevance.

Leaders must continuously monitor DE&I performance metrics, assess the impact of initiatives, and identify areas for adjustment or enhancement. This iterative process ensures that strategies remain aligned with evolving organizational needs, workforce dynamics, and external factors. Just as a product must adapt to changing market demands, DE&I efforts must be responsive to feedback, new insights, and shifting priorities to sustain their effectiveness.

The goal is not only to correct minor oversights but also to seize opportunities for significant advancements, driving greater inclusivity, equity, and engagement. By committing to a culture of continuous improvement, organizations can ensure that their DE&I initiatives remain a dynamic and integral part of their overall success strategy.

## Anticipate and Address Roadblocks

A well-designed strategic plan anticipates potential roadblocks and includes strategies to address them. One of the most common challenges DE&I leaders face is time and executive expectations. Senior leaders often expect cultural change to happen quickly. However, these leaders may not fully appreciate how long it took to establish the existing culture—and how much time is required to shift it.

It's critical to communicate to leadership that cultural transformation requires patience, persistence, and a long-term perspective. This is why a 3- to 5-year plan is ideal for achieving meaningful returns on DE&I investments. Breaking down your goals into manageable steps—limiting the number of initiatives to five to seven—makes them more achievable.

Remember: Rome wasn't built in a day. Changing corporate culture is no different. It requires time to deploy initiatives, assess their impact, and revise them as necessary. Unrealistic expectations will only lead to frustration. By taking a long-term approach, you set your organization up for sustainable success.

By treating DE&I planning with the same discipline as product development, organizations can create inclusive cultures that drive meaningful change and align with evolving workforce demands. The product development cycle has taught us that success doesn't happen by chance. It requires intentionality, thorough planning, and a commitment to continuous improvement.

# Actionable Strategy 1

# Actionable Strategy #1:
# Integrate DE&I into Core Business Strategies

Future-focused leaders understand that embedding DE&I into the DNA of their organization is a business imperative for long-term success. When DE&I becomes a core part of an organization's culture, it influences decision-making, product development, and day-to-day operations. It moves beyond mere compliance to become a central pillar of business strategy.

DE&I should not be confined to Human Resources or Operations alone, nor should the responsibility fall solely on a Chief Diversity Officer or someone with a "Diversity" title. Instead, every business unit must share accountability for driving DE&I outcomes. This shared responsibility ensures that no single department bears the burden of cultural transformation and that DE&I is fully integrated into the company's broader strategic objectives.

## DE&I as a Driver of Business Objectives

Embedding DE&I into the organization's strategic framework strengthens its ability to achieve key objectives while fostering an inclusive workplace. For example, if a company's business goal is to increase market share, DE&I can play a pivotal role in achieving that outcome. Companies can enhance or modify existing products or services to address a specific need of consumers from marginalized communities. This approach not only broadens the customer base but also strengthens brand reputation and differentiates the company in a competitive marketplace.

To do this effectively, companies must avoid superficial efforts that result in reputational damage or accusations of performative allyship. Instead, companies should engage experts who have lived experience within the target demographic or possess deep knowledge of the community's needs. These experts provide critical insights to help companies:

- Design products that address the needs of underserved markets.
- Tailor marketing messages to resonate with the target community.
- Build authentic connections with the community through meaningful engagement.

Companies that attempt to market to marginalized communities without consulting experts often miss the mark. Engaging these communities early, gathering insights, and creating solutions that genuinely address their needs can help organizations avoid costly mistakes and build brand loyalty.

## Cross-Functional Collaboration is Critical

To achieve this level of impact, participation is required from multiple departments. Development, Marketing, Operations, and Sales must collaborate and recognize themselves as key stakeholders in building a more inclusive organization. Offering inclusive products and services to a diverse marketplace isn't just about "doing the right thing"; it drives innovation, market differentiation, and customer loyalty, all of which contribute to long-term profitability.

When DE&I becomes a core business strategy, it fuels growth, strengthens brand loyalty, and positions companies as market leaders. Companies that thrive in the future of work will be those that recognize DE&I not as a side initiative, but as a key lever for growth, innovation, and sustainable profitability.

**Key Points to Consider:**

- Research your competitors' DE&I initiatives. How are they creating more inclusive and accessible products/services? What can you do to differentiate your offerings?
- Establish a DE&I task force that actively participates in the development of your products and services. Include these stakeholders at multiple stages to ensure inclusivity and accessibility are baked into the process.
- Track and communicate outcomes to your workforce. Celebrate successes, but also be transparent about missteps. Sharing lessons learned from failed interventions builds trust and shows a commitment to continual improvement.

# Actionable Strategy 2

# Actionable Strategy #2: Leverage Data for DE&I Success

Organizations have access to a wealth of employee data, yet many fail to leverage it effectively. When combined with direct employee feedback, this data offers critical insights that can drive the creation of more inclusive and equitable workplace cultures. To truly understand the needs of the workforce, leaders must analyze data from multiple perspectives.

## Start with a Comprehensive Assessment

Before embarking on a DE&I journey, it is essential to understand where your organization currently stands. Conducting a comprehensive assessment involves gathering employee feedback through surveys, listening sessions, and other engagement channels. These touchpoints provide a clear picture of employee experiences, revealing areas where inequities may exist.

These data points serve as a foundation for making data-driven decisions about which DE&I interventions to prioritize. To gain a holistic view, organizations must examine data in both aggregate and disaggregated forms. Looking at data in the aggregate offers a broad perspective, but disaggregating it reveals disparities within specific groups. This is where the real insights emerge.

## Go Beyond Basic Demographics

Traditional demographic breakdowns like race, ethnicity, and gender are important, but they don't tell the whole story. To gain deeper insights, companies must explore intersectional identities—the unique experiences that arise from the combination of multiple marginalized identities.

For example, consider the experience of a white female employee who is a single mother caring for aging parents, compared to a white female employee who is married with no children. While they share the same race and gender, their lived experiences within the workplace are markedly different. Intersectionality matters. By taking this approach, companies can identify the specific challenges faced by different employee groups and design targeted interventions to address them.

## Data Collection Should Be Continuous, Not One-Time

Because the employee population is constantly changing—whether through new hires, exits, or changes in employee needs—DE&I assessments must be ongoing. While annual employee surveys provide a solid foundation, organizations should also incorporate more frequent, short surveys—often called pulse surveys—which are designed to quickly gauge employee sentiment and gather timely feedback. Feedback sessions can also be conducted as needed to address specific issues or areas of concern. This allows companies to track the success of interventions in real time and make necessary adjustments.

## Make Data-Driven Decisions

When companies leverage employee data strategically, they shift from guessing to knowing. Data-driven decision-making enables leaders to tailor DE&I interventions to the unique needs of their workforce. This approach increases the likelihood of achieving lasting impact.

For example, if employee feedback indicates a lack of psychological safety within a particular department, leaders can target interventions to address it. If disaggregated data reveals disparities in promotion rates for specific groups, leaders can examine hiring and promotion processes for potential bias.

## Closing the Loop on Data-Driven Change

Data collection alone is not enough. Leaders must act on the insights they gather. It's not enough to listen—employees need to see action. When employees see that their feedback is being used to create meaningful change, it builds trust and encourages greater participation in future data collection efforts.

By embracing data-driven DE&I strategies, organizations can:

- Pinpoint inequities that may not be visible at the surface level.
- Develop targeted interventions to address disparities.
- Monitor the effectiveness of those interventions over time.

DE&I initiatives must be more than well-meaning declarations; they must be grounded in data. By using data as a strategic tool, organizations can design interventions that address real challenges, not assumptions. Data-driven DE&I is intentional, targeted, and customized to meet the specific needs of the workforce. When done right, it leads to more inclusive workplaces where all employees feel seen, valued, and supported.

## Key Points to Consider:

- HR Data Analytics: Consider creating roles specifically designed to analyze HR data in ways that support DE&I decision-making. This will help leaders make data-informed interventions.

- Employee Lifecycle Assessments: Continuously assess key stages of the employee journey, from onboarding to training and exit. Gather feedback at each stage to understand how employees experience the organization and its culture.
- Recruitment and Interview Process Feedback: Collect feedback from all candidates, including those who were not offered positions, to improve your recruitment and talent management processes.
- Career Advancement Data: Track the career progression of high-potential employees across different groups to identify disparities in promotion and advancement. Use this data to ensure all employees have equal opportunities for growth.
- Addressing Disparities: If disparities are identified, it gives you a legitimate business reason to implement targeted DE&I interventions. Data-backed actions are less likely to face resistance and scrutiny.

# Actionable Strategy 3

# Actionable Strategy #3:
# Track and Measure DE&I Progress

The popular management principle, *"What gets measured gets done,"* holds especially true for DE&I initiatives. Many organizations struggle to advance inclusion and equity because they either fail to measure progress effectively or aren't clear on what to measure. Not knowing how to articulate what success looks like is a surefire way not to know what it is when you achieve it. Defining specific, measurable outcomes is essential, and setting SMART goals (Specific, Measurable, Achievable, Realistic, and Time-bound) is the best way to achieve that.

Crafting SMART goals can sometimes be challenging. Here is an example of a SMART goal for one's recruiting organization:

Increase by 20% **[Measurable]** the representation of candidates from underrepresented groups (e.g., women, BIPOC [Black, Indigenous, People of Color], individuals with disabilities, LGBTQ, and veterans) **[Specific]** in the candidate pool for all open requisitions, with candidate pool composition measured at key hiring milestones (e.g., 14, 21, and 30 days) **[Timebound]** to ensure equity in sourcing.

Although not explicitly stated, this goal is also achievable and realistic, as it sets a clear, data-driven target that can be monitored at specific intervals. By aligning with the SMART framework, this goal provides clarity, accountability, and a clear path to progress.

## Make Measurement a Continuous Process

Tracking DE&I initiatives should be a continuous effort—not a one-time evaluation. Consistent monitoring allows leaders to assess progress, identify gaps, and make real-time adjustments. Year-over-year reviews provide a comprehensive view of momentum, highlight areas of improvement, and reveal where further support may be needed. Without continuous measurement, it's difficult to determine whether interventions are having a lasting impact.

To maintain visibility and accountability, companies can leverage tools such as:

- Dashboards to visualize critical metrics, such as employee demographics, hiring and promotion rates, and sentiment scores from employee engagement surveys.
- Employee Net Promoter Score (eNPS) summaries to measure employee satisfaction and engagement.
- Employee impact reports that highlight key data trends and action items for leadership.

Sharing this data in company-wide meetings, internal newsletters, or on a DE&I portal creates transparency and strengthens trust between leadership and employees. When employees see that their input is being used to shape workplace improvements, they become more engaged.

At the end of each year—or at the conclusion of a DE&I strategic plan—companies should conduct a SWOT analysis (Strengths, Weaknesses, Opportunities, and Threats) to assess progress, identify risks, and recalibrate as needed. This process helps ensure that DE&I strategies remain flexible, actionable, and aligned with workforce needs and market demands.

## Build Transparency and Trust

Employees want to know how their company is progressing on its DE&I journey and, more importantly, how those efforts impact their daily work experiences. Transparency builds trust and credibility. When companies openly share the results of their DE&I efforts, employees are more likely to remain engaged, provide honest feedback, and contribute to continuous improvement.

However, transparency without follow-through can backfire. If leaders share the results of an employee survey but fail to act on the feedback, employees may become disillusioned. To prevent this, leaders must close the feedback loop by announcing the actions they plan to take in response to employee feedback. This can be as simple as an internal memo, a town hall meeting, or a message from senior leadership that outlines key changes and upcoming initiatives.

When employees see that their feedback has led to real change, it builds trust and encourages further engagement. Companies should establish a feedback-action-feedback cycle where updates on progress are shared consistently. The simple act of telling employees, *"Here's what we learned, here's what we're doing about it, and here's how you'll see the impact,"* reinforces the company's commitment to DE&I.

## Track Progress, But Be Flexible

Measuring success is critical, but so is course correction. Not every DE&I intervention will have the desired impact, and that's okay. The goal is to track progress, evaluate the effectiveness of interventions, and refine strategies as needed. Companies that commit to ongoing reflection and recalibration are better positioned to achieve sustainable, long-term success.

For example, suppose a company launches a mentorship program and tracks promotion rates for mentees compared to non-mentees. If the data reveals that mentees aren't being promoted at higher rates, leaders should analyze the program's design to identify gaps. Are mentors equipped with the right resources to support mentees? Are mentees being given access to high-visibility projects and stretch assignments? Instead of abandoning the initiative, companies should refine the program, re-test it, and track new results.

Flexibility and agility are essential because DE&I work is dynamic. Changes in employee demographics, industry regulations, and workforce expectations may require a re-evaluation of goals. Organizations that remain adaptable, responsive, and committed to continuous learning will see greater returns on their DE&I investments.

## Keep Leadership Accountable

Accountability is crucial for maintaining momentum. While DE&I leaders, Chief People Officers, and executive sponsors play a key role, accountability shouldn't fall solely on them. DE&I success requires shared responsibility across all business units. Leaders from every department—whether in marketing, sales, or operations—must see themselves as stakeholders in the success of DE&I.

Accountability mechanisms might include:

- Quarterly check-ins with executive sponsors and business unit leaders to review progress and adjust strategies.
- Public dashboards that track key DE&I metrics and report them to employees.

- Annual DE&I impact reports that highlight wins, challenges, and forward-looking strategies.

Companies can also incorporate DE&I goals into executive performance reviews, linking them directly to executive bonuses or compensation. When senior leaders are incentivized to meet DE&I targets, they're more likely to prioritize them.

## Practical Tips for Tracking and Measuring DE&I

1. **Make measurement part of your business operations.** Use dashboards, employee impact reports, and eNPS scores to monitor key metrics.
2. **Close the feedback loop.** Share updates on employee feedback and explain how the company is responding.
3. **Be transparent.** Create a DE&I portal where employees can see the company's progress in real time.
4. **Incorporate DE&I goals into performance reviews.** When executives and managers are held accountable for DE&I, they prioritize it.
5. **Don't wait for perfection.** Track progress continuously, refine initiatives, and remain flexible when interventions fall short of expectations.

Tracking and measuring DE&I progress is essential for driving meaningful, sustainable change. Companies must treat DE&I like any other business objective—setting SMART goals, tracking progress, and holding stakeholders accountable. By leveraging tools like dashboards, eNPS (employee net promoter scores) surveys, and employee impact reports, companies can assess impact, ensure transparency, and course-correct as needed.

But data alone is not enough. Companies must act on what the data reveals. Regular reflection, flexibility, and accountability keep DE&I efforts on track. When organizations consistently track and measure their DE&I efforts, they build trust with employees, strengthen workplace culture, and position themselves for sustainable growth.

## Key Points to Consider:

- Set SMART DE&I goals (specific, measurable, achievable, realistic, and time-bound) and assign stakeholders responsible for championing these efforts.
- Identify potential challenges and develop mitigation strategies to overcome obstacles.
- Conduct annual SWOT analyses (Strengths, Weaknesses, Opportunities, and Threats) to assess progress and recalibrate strategies as needed.
- Communicate findings transparently—celebrate successes, share missteps, and explain lessons learned from unsuccessful interventions.

# Reflection Questions

- How can you more effectively align DE&I initiatives with broader business objectives to drive innovation, market expansion, or operational efficiency?
- What specific, measurable changes do you aim to see in your workforce or operations as a result of DE&I strategies? (e.g., improved retention, increased employee satisfaction, or better product innovation)
- How will DE&I contribute to your organization's long-term legacy, brand equity, and industry reputation?
- What specific actions can you take in the next 30, 60, or 90 days to leverage DE&I as a competitive advantage? (Consider your approach to talent acquisition, employee engagement, product development, and customer trust.)

_____

_____

_____

_____

_____

_____

Strategically embedding DE&I into your organizational structure requires intentionality and collaboration between leadership and the workforce. Effectively leveraging tools and resources is essential to fostering truly inclusive workplace cultures. In the next chapter, we will explore how AI and machine learning can be harnessed not only to enhance business efficiency but also to drive equity and inclusion throughout the organization.

# Chapter 2:
# Harnessing Technology and AI for Inclusivity

> *"Whether AI will help us reach our aspirations or reinforce the unjust inequalities is ultimately up to us."*
>
> — ***Joy Buolamwini***

The proliferation of artificial intelligence (AI) tools and machine learning (ML) technologies is transforming the way we work. These tools are designed to increase efficiency, enhance productivity, and position organizations to innovate and meet evolving market demands. However, employees are rightfully concerned that AI may replace human jobs—and there is merit to this concern.

According to Goldman Sachs, AI is projected to replace 300 million full-time jobs globally.[3] Similarly, the McKinsey Global Institute estimates that 12 million employees will need to change professions by 2030.[4] Historically, technology has always driven change in the job market, often displacing manual labor with more efficient, cost-effective solutions. AI is no exception—tasks that are repetitive, tedious, and rules-based will likely be automated by AI-powered tools. However, this shift also creates opportunities for employees to focus on more strategic, innovative work that AI cannot replicate.

## The Knowledge Gap on AI's Capabilities

Many corporate leaders have a limited understanding of AI's capabilities and how to leverage its evolving potential effectively. Without a clear AI strategy, some leaders adopt a short-sighted approach—replacing employees with AI tools to achieve short-term gains. While this approach may yield immediate cost savings, it is unlikely to result in long-term success. The reality is that while the

---

[3] Goldman Sachs. (2023, April 5). *Generative AI could raise global GDP by 7%.* Goldman Sachs Insights. Retrieved from https://www.goldmansachs.com/insights/articles/generative-ai-could-raise-global-gdp-by-7-percent

[4] McKinsey Global Institute. (2024, January 20). *Generative AI and the future of work in America*. Retrieved from https://www.mckinsey.com/mgi/our-research/generative-ai-and-the-future-of-work-in-america

nature of work will continue to evolve, human insight, judgment, and creativity will remain essential to business operations. Leaders who recognize this truth will be better positioned to navigate the future of work.

To successfully integrate AI, companies must be strategic. They must either hire new talent with specialized skills in AI or, more strategically, upskill or reskill existing employees to work alongside AI technologies. Upskilling current employees has the dual benefit of preserving institutional knowledge and building internal capacity for innovation. This approach strengthens organizational agility while fostering employee loyalty and retention.

## The Shift from Replacement to Collaboration

The most forward-thinking leaders recognize that AI is not a replacement for human talent but an enabler of human potential. Rather than seeing AI as a threat, they view it as a co-pilot that can support human decision-making, reduce workload, and streamline processes. This shift requires foresight, intentional planning, and ongoing learning for both leaders and employees.

Employers must offer ongoing learning and development opportunities, while employees must take the initiative to acquire new skills and adapt to the demands of a changing workplace. This continuous learning cycle ensures that employees remain employable in an AI-driven world. But upskilling employees is only part of the equation. Leaders must also prioritize the ethical and responsible use of AI, ensuring that its deployment is aligned with organizational goals and industry standards.

## Responsible, Ethical, and Transparent AI

The integration of AI tools requires more than technical know-how; it requires a governance framework grounded in three foundational principles:

1. **Responsible AI** – AI systems must be thoughtfully designed and deployed to minimize risk and unintended harm. Responsible AI considers the broader impact on stakeholders, ensuring that its implementation aligns with the company's mission, values, and long-term business goals.
2. **Ethical AI** – Ethical AI ensures fairness and actively works to prevent the introduction of bias. Bias in AI can result in discriminatory outcomes, especially in recruitment, performance management, and promotion decisions. Ethical AI ensures that all system outputs are fair, equitable, and free from discrimination.
3. **Transparent AI** – Transparency means that AI-driven decisions are explainable, understandable, and defensible. Employees, leaders, and stakeholders must be able to trace how an AI system reached its conclusion. Transparency builds trust and provides accountability for errors or unintended consequences.

These principles are not abstract ideals—they are operational necessities. Companies that fail to prioritize responsible, ethical, and transparent AI risk reputational damage, loss of customer trust, and even legal liability. Organizations must ensure that employees, particularly those who interact with AI tools, are trained in these principles. Employees trained in AI literacy and governance principles will become essential to an organization's long-term success.

## Human Oversight Remains Critical

While AI can perform repetitive, rules-based tasks, it lacks human empathy, creativity, and ethical reasoning. Companies that rely solely on AI-driven decision-making without human oversight expose themselves to significant business risks. For instance, if an AI-powered recruitment tool makes biased hiring decisions, the organization may face reputational harm, legal exposure, and employee dissatisfaction.

Human oversight is essential for maintaining ethical, transparent, and fair AI systems. By creating checks and balances for AI tools, organizations can ensure that these systems operate in alignment with their core values. Companies must integrate human review processes for decisions made by AI, especially in high-stakes areas like recruitment, promotions, and disciplinary actions.

## The Path Forward

The future of work is not about replacing humans with machines—it's about creating a collaborative dynamic where human talent and AI tools work in tandem. By thoughtfully integrating AI and prioritizing responsible, ethical, and transparent governance, organizations can innovate faster, improve decision-making, and build sustainable, inclusive workplace cultures.

AI is a tool for transformation—not displacement. Leaders who understand this distinction will position their companies to thrive in the ever-evolving future of work.

# Actionable Strategy

# 4

Actionable Strategy #4:

Implement Ethical AI Practices

A global survey by McKinsey & Company revealed that the use of Artificial Intelligence (AI) in business operations increased from 55% in 2023 to 72% in 2024, with organizations citing benefits such as increased productivity, improved product and service quality, and faster time-to-market.[5] While the potential benefits are clear, it's equally important to recognize and address the inherent risks.

AI and machine learning (ML) tools are created by humans, and as such, they are susceptible to human biases—both conscious and unconscious—that can be introduced at various stages of the process, including design, development, and training. Without appropriate safeguards, these biases can result in critical vulnerabilities that lead to discrimination, disparate treatment, and inequitable outcomes in both the workplace and the marketplace.

Unlike humans, AI cannot self-identify or self-correct for bias. AI systems are only as unbiased as the people and data used to build them. This is why human oversight is essential at every stage of the AI workflow—from design and development to deployment and monitoring. Without this oversight, organizations risk relying on flawed systems that perpetuate the very inequities they aim to eliminate.

## How to Mitigate Bias in AI Development

One of the most effective ways to mitigate bias during the development phase is to diversify development teams. The teams responsible for designing, developing, and training AI-powered tools

---

[5] McKinsey & Company. (2024, May 30). *The state of AI in early 2024: Gen AI adoption spikes, starts to generate value.* QuantumBlack AI. Retrieved from https://www.mckinsey.com/capabilities/quantumblack/our-insights/the-state-of-ai

should reflect a broad range of identities, abilities, and lived experiences. Diverse perspectives help to identify blind spots that homogeneous teams may overlook. This is especially important during data collection and training, as the datasets used to train AI models must also be inclusive and representative of the populations the system is intended to serve.

When datasets lack diversity, AI systems are more likely to produce biased outcomes. For example, an AI hiring tool trained on resumes from a predominantly male workforce may "learn" to favor male candidates, even when gender is not an explicitly coded factor. Ensuring that training datasets reflect a diverse range of experiences, identities, and conditions is essential to building fairer AI systems.

## For Companies Procuring AI Tools

When procuring AI tools from third-party vendors, partnering with those committed to responsible and ethical AI practices is essential. The procurement process should include thorough due diligence to ensure vendors prioritize fairness, ethical design, and compliance with data privacy standards.

AI tools often require access to sensitive employee data, creating potential risks for security breaches and misuse. To address these concerns, companies must ensure that vendors adhere to privacy frameworks such as the California Consumer Privacy Act (CCPA) and the General Data Protection Regulation (GDPR). Compliance with these frameworks safeguards personal data and reduces the likelihood of legal and reputational risks associated with AI use.

## AI Vendor Requirements

To ensure AI tools are procured with ethical and responsible principles in mind, consider the following actions:

- **Request Governance Protocols:**

Ask vendors to provide their internal AI governance protocols. These should include clear steps for identifying and mitigating bias, correcting issues, and retraining AI systems when necessary. Transparent governance frameworks are a foundation for ensuring ethical AI usage.

- **Demand Case Studies on Inclusivity:**

Require vendors to share case studies that demonstrate how their AI tools perform across diverse demographic groups and use cases. This ensures the tools are tested for fairness and effectiveness in varied environments, not just among a narrow subset of users.

- **Request AI Literacy Training:**

Vendors should offer AI literacy training for your team. Employees need a foundational understanding of how AI systems work, how to monitor them for bias, and how to escalate issues for resolution. This empowers your organization to use AI responsibly and effectively.

- **Conduct Regular Audits:**

Insist that vendors perform regular audits of their AI tools. As AI systems evolve, updates and retraining can inadvertently introduce new biases. Periodic reviews ensure the system continues to operate ethically and remains aligned with your organization's expectations.

By prioritizing these practices during procurement, your organization can mitigate the risks associated with bias in AI systems while ensuring tools are both ethical and effective. This proactive approach safeguards data privacy, enhances trust, and strengthens your company's commitment to fairness and inclusivity in the workplace.

## Establishing AI Governance

As discussed in the previous section, AI governance is critical for mitigating bias in AI-powered tools. Governance provides a clear framework for how AI tools are built, tested, and deployed. It also establishes the roles, responsibilities, and accountability mechanisms needed to ensure fairness and transparency.

Key elements of an effective AI governance framework include:

- **Fairness Protocols**: Formalize procedures for bias detection and mitigation at every stage of AI development. This should include how datasets are sourced, labeled, and used.
- **Accountability Structures**: Define roles and responsibilities for human oversight, ensuring there are dedicated team members tasked with reviewing and challenging AI-generated decisions.
- **Ethics Committees**: Form an ethics review board or committee responsible for assessing AI system performance, particularly in high-impact areas like hiring, promotion, and pay equity.
- **Transparent Reporting**: Establish a system for documenting and reporting on AI tool performance, including the frequency and outcomes of audits. Transparent reporting builds employee trust and provides accountability.

## The Role of Employee Training in Mitigating AI Bias

Effective AI governance requires more than well-designed systems; it requires AI-literate employees. Employees who interact with AI tools—whether in hiring, customer service, or data analysis—must be trained to recognize signs of bias and understand how to intervene. Companies should provide AI ethics training as part of their broader learning and development efforts.

Through training, employees learn to identify:

- **Red flags**: Unexpected patterns in AI-generated outputs that may suggest bias or inaccuracies.
- **Decision pathways**: How AI systems make decisions, allowing employees to challenge those decisions when inconsistencies arise.
- **Reporting protocols**: How to report suspected bias and escalate issues to appropriate stakeholders for review and remediation.

Training employees in ethical AI use creates an additional layer of protection for the organization, ensuring employees are equipped to detect and address potential risks.

## The Business Case for Mitigating AI Bias

The business case for responsible AI practices goes beyond compliance—it's a matter of risk mitigation, brand reputation, and operational efficiency. Without human oversight and responsible governance, organizations face:

- **Legal Liability**: If AI-driven employment decisions result in discriminatory outcomes, organizations could face lawsuits or regulatory scrutiny.

- **Reputational Damage**: News of AI bias spreads quickly. Publicized cases of AI bias have led to brand backlash and calls for boycotts.
- **Loss of Talent**: Employees who experience or witness bias caused by AI tools may lose trust in the organization, leading to turnover.

On the flip side, organizations that prioritize responsible, ethical, and transparent AI enjoy several business benefits:

- **Enhanced Brand Reputation**: Companies known for responsible AI practices earn trust from consumers, employees, and investors.
- **Increased Innovation**: Organizations that foster diverse development teams create AI tools that perform well for a broader range of users, unlocking new market opportunities.
- **Regulatory Preparedness**: Governments are developing regulations to oversee AI development and usage. Organizations that prioritize responsible AI practices today will be better prepared for future compliance requirements.

AI systems are transforming how work gets done, but they are not immune to bias. Without appropriate safeguards, AI can perpetuate and exacerbate inequities within organizations. By following responsible AI practices—like diversifying development teams, demanding vendor accountability, and establishing ethical governance protocols—organizations can mitigate these risks.

Human oversight, employee training, and ongoing audits are essential to ensuring that AI tools operate fairly, ethically, and transparently. Companies that prioritize responsible AI design position themselves as leaders in innovation, risk mitigation, and ethical business practices.

## Key Points to Consider:

- **Assume bias exists in every AI tool**: Proactively conduct regular audits to identify, measure, and mitigate bias before it impacts business outcomes.
- **Pinpoint critical stages of vulnerability**: Identify key stages in the design, development, and training process where bias is most likely to emerge, and implement strategies to address it early.
- **Ensure human oversight at every decision point**: Embed human oversight at every stage of the AI workflow, especially in decision-making and predictive processes, to ensure accountability and ethical alignment.

# Actionable Strategy 5

# Actionable Strategy #5: Leverage Technology to Achieve Inclusivity for All Employees

Equitable access to technology goes beyond simply providing employees with a laptop. It means ensuring that every team member has access to the devices, software applications, and resources necessary to perform their job effectively. Achieving this requires a deeper understanding of the diverse needs of your workforce and a commitment to tailoring technological solutions accordingly.

For example, an employee with a disability may require assistive technologies, such as voice command software, screen readers, or alternative input devices, to work efficiently. Similarly, employees for whom English is a second language may benefit from translation software or tools that allow them to work in their native language while producing outputs in English. These accommodations empower employees to work more effectively and contribute to the organization's overall success.

To accurately assess the technological needs of your workforce, direct engagement with employees is essential—never make assumptions about what they may need. One effective approach is to integrate this process into your onboarding experience. During onboarding, engage in a conversation with new hires to outline the standard technological devices, resources, and tools typically provided to employees. This is an opportunity to ask if these tools will meet their needs or if additional resources are required for them to thrive in their new role. For instance, an employee may disclose that they are neurodivergent or have an invisible disability and may require assistive technology or other accommodations. Creating space for this dialogue allows you to proactively support employees from day one.

Additionally, collaboration with your IT team can help you identify opportunities to optimize existing technologies for accessibility and inclusivity. This may involve exploring software updates, plug-ins, or new devices that better meet the needs of all employees, not just those who disclose a need for support. Consider auditing your current technology stack to identify areas for improvement.

Your goal should be to provide tools and resources that meet functional needs while promoting a culture of inclusivity and accessibility. By actively supporting employees with the right technology, you enable them to perform at their best, drive productivity, and foster an equitable workplace where all employees feel supported and valued.

## Key Points to Consider:

- Enable closed captioning on platforms like Microsoft Teams or Zoom during meetings to ensure all employees, including those who are deaf or hard of hearing, can access shared information.
- Encourage employees to turn on their cameras during virtual meetings, as this supports employees who rely on lip-reading for effective communication.
- Provide standing desks to promote employees' overall health, comfort, and well-being, recognizing the impact of ergonomics on long-term productivity.
- Offer audio recording tools to support employees with limited mobility or dexterity, enabling them to capture thoughts, draft documents, or document processes efficiently.

- Leverage generative AI tools to support editing, proofreading, and content development, enhancing efficiency and performance for all employees, especially those with neurodivergent thinking styles or language barriers.

These recommendations foster an inclusive and accessible environment for both in-office and remote employees, ensuring that all employees have equitable access to the resources they need to thrive in their roles.

# Reflection Questions

- What AI tools are currently in use or planned for procurement that may require employee retraining or upskilling?
- How can you audit and adjust your AI systems to reduce the presence of bias and ensure equitable outcomes?
- Are there any gaps in your employees' access to essential technology, tools, or resources required for their role?
- What immediate changes can you implement within the next 30, 60, or 90 days to enhance accessibility and inclusivity in your workplace?

While AI and technology can enhance productivity and help reduce bias when managed properly, the human element of leadership remains essential. Next, we'll focus on building a diverse and inclusive leadership pipeline that reflects the evolving workforce and promotes equity at all levels of your organization.

# Chapter 3:
# Building Inclusive Leadership Pipeline for the Future

> *"Leadership is not about being in charge. It is about taking care of those in your charge."*
>
> — ***Simon Sinek***

An inclusive leadership pipeline begins with intentional, inclusive hiring practices. A recruitment strategy that actively sources talent from diverse networks, communities, schools, and the military while prioritizing candidates with transferable skills is critical for building a diverse candidate pool. However, a common obstacle to achieving this goal is bias.

Bias can appear in various forms—such as preferences for candidates from specific schools or former employers—or it can be embedded in AI recruiting software that relies on keywords or proxies (like names, zip codes, or employment gaps) to exclude marginalized groups. AI tools trained with biased datasets may inadvertently screen out qualified candidates, perpetuating inequities. To address this critical vulnerability, designate someone on your recruiting team to review decisions made by AI systems, ensuring qualified candidates are not being excluded. AI should enhance decision-making, not replace human judgment.

Bias can also arise during the interview process. To mitigate this, educate interviewers on how to recognize and avoid bias. Develop a standardized set of interview questions for all candidates and use a scoring rubric to evaluate responses. These measures reduce subjectivity, foster consistency, and create a fairer decision-making process.

Creating a workforce that reflects diverse identities and lived experiences is only the first step. Building a truly inclusive leadership pipeline requires deliberate succession planning and career development initiatives. This begins with empowering managers to support employees' growth within the organization.

## Individual Development Plans (IDPs): The Foundation for Growth

Managers should engage employees in regular discussions about their Individual Development Plans (IDPs). These plans identify areas for personal growth, skills to develop, and potential career paths. Effective managers proactively help employees acquire the skills and training necessary to explore opportunities and advance their careers.

## Succession Planning: Preparing for the Future

Succession planning is a collaborative effort between managers and employees to chart career paths within the organization. Managers must identify skill or knowledge gaps and work with employees to bridge them through training, mentorship, or project assignments. For succession planning to be meaningful, equity must be at the forefront. Train managers to recognize and address their biases when assessing promotion eligibility or assigning developmental opportunities.

## Equity in Growth Opportunities

Particular attention should be given to traditionally underrepresented groups, as they may require additional support to access growth and leadership opportunities. Equitable distribution of special projects, which are often used to gauge leadership potential, is critical. Without access to these opportunities, employees from marginalized groups may be overlooked, undermining the value of your succession plan.

These assignments are more than just tasks; they allow employees to showcase their capabilities, gain visibility, and build the competencies necessary for advancement. By ensuring that these opportunities are distributed fairly, organizations can create a leadership pipeline that reflects their commitment to equity and inclusion.

By fostering inclusive hiring practices, robust career development, and equitable succession planning, organizations can build a leadership pipeline that is not only diverse but also inclusive—positioning themselves for sustainable success in the future of work.

# Actionable Strategy 6

# Actionable Strategy #6:
# Invest in Inclusive Leadership Training

Today's leaders must be equipped to manage an increasingly diverse, multigenerational, intersectional, and often hybrid or remote workforce. Leading such a dynamic team requires more than traditional management skills; it demands a deep understanding of Diversity, Equity, and Inclusion (DE&I) principles and the ability to apply them effectively in real-world scenarios.

Ensuring that leaders understand DE&I principles—and why they are integral to your organization—benefits both individual leaders and the company as a whole. This understanding fosters greater engagement, alignment with company goals, and improved team dynamics. However, resistance to these principles is not uncommon. Such resistance presents an opportunity for senior leaders to assess whether individuals who oppose DE&I efforts can effectively contribute to operational success.

Leaders who are self-aware, culturally competent, and skilled at building trust through open and authentic communication are better positioned to support organizational objectives. Effective communication is central to fostering an inclusive workplace culture. Leaders must not only communicate with respect but also inspire, motivate, and hold their teams accountable.

Unfortunately, these critical skills are not typically included in the training managers receive when they transition into people management roles—but they should be. The days of relying solely on basic online training modules that merely teach managers not to discriminate or harass are long gone. Today's leaders must learn how to manage people who think differently, communicate differently, and bring diverse perspectives to the workplace. If managers are to help employees perform at their best, they must engage with their teams in more inclusive and meaningful ways.

Developing inclusive leadership now requires a commitment to continuous learning and self-improvement. Leaders should actively seek experiences that challenge them, broaden their perspectives, and deepen their understanding of DE&I principles.

This can include:

- **Participating in Employee Resource Groups (ERGs):** Learning directly from colleagues with different identities and lived experiences offers invaluable insights.
- **Attending Conferences:** Being in spaces where they are in the minority provides leaders with a deeper understanding of the challenges faced by underrepresented groups.
- **Enrolling in Leadership Development Programs:** Programs focusing on cultural competence, delivered through cohort-based training, create safe environments for leaders to discuss experiences, ask questions, and grow.

## Key Points to Consider:

- **Master Communication Skills:** Equip leaders with the tools to foster an inclusive and psychologically safe workplace culture.
- **Engage Qualified Trainers:** Seek out corporate trainers with the expertise needed to instill inclusive leadership qualities within your organization.

- **Ensure Accountability:** Hold managers accountable for supporting the development and advancement of all employees, particularly those from marginalized groups.
- **Support Employee Advancement:** Hold managers accountable for promoting equity and career growth for employees, especially those from marginalized groups.

By investing in leadership training that prioritizes inclusivity, organizations can build a culture of belonging, improve team performance, and create a leadership pipeline ready to meet the challenges of the future of work.

# Actionable Strategy 7

# Actionable Strategy #7:
# Create Career Pathways through Mentorship and Sponsorship

The notion that success can be achieved solely by "pulling oneself up by their bootstraps" is a myth. Most successful leaders have benefited from mentors or sponsors who mentioned their names in key conversations, connected them to valuable networks, or provided opportunities they wouldn't have otherwise accessed. These vital connections are often inaccessible to individuals from marginalized identities. Implementing mentorship and sponsorship programs helps bridge this gap, creating opportunities that benefit both employees and the organization as a whole.

Opportunities for career advancement frequently emerge in informal settings, such as in-office meetings, networking events, or after-hours gatherings—spaces where not all employees are present or even aware. This creates inherent inequities in access to opportunities. To address this disparity, establishing mentorship and sponsorship programs is critical for leveling the playing field.

**Mentorship Programs:** Mentors guide employees by helping them navigate workplace dynamics, sharing insights about organizational culture, and offering advice based on their own experiences. A mentor typically has credibility within the organization and can help mentees integrate effectively and build confidence in their roles.

**Sponsorship Programs:** Sponsors, on the other hand, are influential leaders who have built significant social capital within the organization. Unlike mentors, sponsors actively advocate for their protégés. They endorse them in high-level discussions, promote their visibility in important spaces, and facilitate access to career-advancing opportunities. Sponsors use their influence to propel their protégés' careers forward.

While these programs can be made available to all employees, they are especially impactful for individuals from traditionally underrepresented groups. Providing access to mentorship and sponsorship ensures these employees gain the guidance and opportunities they might otherwise miss due to exclusion from informal networks prevalent in corporate cultures.

## Key Points to Consider:

- **Implement a Mentorship Program:** Pair junior employees with experienced mentors to help them navigate the organization and develop professionally.
- **Establish a Sponsorship Program:** Identify high-potential employees and pair them with senior leaders who can actively advocate for their advancement.
- **Ensure Inclusivity:** Make these programs accessible to all employees, particularly those from underrepresented groups. Develop objective criteria for participation and secure commitments from both mentors and mentees or sponsors and protégés.
- **Promote Awareness:** Educate employees about the availability and benefits of mentorship and sponsorship programs, encouraging participation across all levels of the organization.
- **Regularly Evaluate:** Continuously assess the effectiveness of these programs by gathering feedback from participants and adjusting strategies to maximize their impact.

## Reflection Questions

- What strategies can you implement to build effective mentorship programs within your organization?
- How can you foster inclusive leadership through targeted training?
- What steps can you take to improve communication practices to ensure all employees feel supported and valued?

_____

_____

_____

_____

_____

_____

_____

_____

_____

_____

Effective leadership is essential to fostering an inclusive culture, but adapting leadership approaches to a dynamic and evolving workforce is equally important. In the following chapter, we'll explore how leaders can create inclusive work environments that thrive in remote and hybrid settings.

# Chapter 4:
# Adapting to a Dynamic Workforce

> *"The future of work is about flexibility, diversity, and empowerment."*
>
> — *Arianna Huffington*

*I*n March 2020, the world changed forever. The coronavirus disease of 2019 (COVID-19), a highly infectious virus, caused severe respiratory symptoms and claimed the lives of over one million people in the United States alone. Transmitted through close contact with infected individuals, the risk of exposure was exceptionally high. To mitigate the spread, government officials implemented strict lockdowns, requiring people to stay home, with only essential workers permitted to leave for work or other critical needs.

The COVID-19 pandemic forced corporations to address a dual challenge: maintaining business operations while safeguarding the health and well-being of their workforce. Although workplace safety has always been a priority, the pandemic redefined what it meant to protect employees, given the scale of the crisis and the global loss of life.

Suddenly, jobs that had never been considered for remote work transitioned to virtual models out of necessity. Employees were rapidly equipped with the tools and resources needed to work from home. However, not everyone could make this transition. Essential workers—whose jobs required them to be on-site or in the field—continued working in person, often facing heightened risks to their health and safety.

## Navigating the Post-Pandemic Workforce Landscape

Now, in a post-pandemic era, corporate leaders are grappling with a transformed workforce landscape. Many are questioning whether to mandate employees' return to the office or adapt to the flexible work models that emerged during the pandemic.

Some leaders have acknowledged that the proverbial genie is out of the bottle—recognizing the difficulties of mandating full-time, in-office attendance. They've realized that remote work can be just as effective, if not more so, and provides opportunities to maintain productivity while reducing overhead costs by forgoing expensive office leases.

Others argue that productivity, collaboration, and team dynamics suffer without physical proximity. In response, many organizations are exploring hybrid work models, allowing employees to split their time between home and office. However, there remain leaders who resist change altogether, mandating a full return to the office despite growing demands from employees for flexibility.

## Balancing Flexibility, Productivity, and Costs

Striking the right balance between maintaining productivity, reducing costs, and meeting employee expectations is one of the most critical challenges organizations face today. Companies that successfully navigate these competing interests will be better positioned to thrive in the evolving world of work.

The most innovative companies recognize that remote and flexible work options are no longer a perk—they are a demand. Today's employees seek workplaces that align with their shifting values, such as work-life balance, flexibility, and autonomy. Embracing these expectations is not just about adapting to workforce trends; it's about fostering a work environment that attracts and retains top talent, drives innovation, and positions companies as leaders in this new era of work.

## A New Era of Work

In this dynamic landscape, flexibility has become a cornerstone of organizational success. Companies that cling to outdated models risk alienating their workforce, losing competitive advantages, and falling behind. In contrast, those that embrace a dynamic, people-centered approach will be the ones that define the future of work.

# Actionable Strategy 8

# Actionable Strategy #8:
# Cultivate Inclusivity in Remote and Hybrid Teams

Hybrid and remote work models are now permanent fixtures in today's workforce, offering both opportunities and challenges. Research shows that employees working remotely at least two days per week are just as productive as their in-office peers.[6] The real challenge lies in fostering inclusive and connected environments that support diverse work structures.

## Addressing Productivity Concerns

Productivity concerns are valid, but decisions should be data-driven, not based on anecdotal evidence. Each job function has unique requirements—some roles demand an on-site presence due to the nature of the work, while others excel in fully remote setups. Leaders must assess these differences and evaluate productivity through measurable performance metrics, such as outcomes, deliverables, and goal achievement, rather than implementing blanket policies that may not fit every role.

For example, instead of mandating a full return to the office because a few roles struggle with remote work, leaders should address specific challenges directly. This approach ensures interventions are targeted, fair, and effective, avoiding unnecessary disruption for roles that function well remotely.

Building a people-first culture requires trust. Trusting employees to meet expectations—regardless of where they work—fosters

---

[6] Crawford, K. (2024, June 12). *Hybrid work is a "win-win" for companies, workers, study finds.* Stanford Institute for Economic Policy Research (SIEPR). Retrieved from https://siepr.stanford.edu/news/hybrid-work-win-win-win-companies-workers-study-finds

engagement and accountability. If productivity issues arise or trust is broken, leaders should address the root cause with thoughtful, targeted interventions. Solutions might include improving communication tools, clarifying expectations, or providing additional resources, all while preserving inclusivity and avoiding rigid mandates that could harm morale.

## The Manager's Role in Cultivating Inclusivity

Managers play a pivotal role in creating inclusive work cultures for hybrid and remote teams. Whether employees are fully remote, hybrid, or in-office, it is the manager's responsibility to ensure everyone feels included, valued, and appreciated. Physical proximity can no longer be the foundation for collaboration and engagement.

Here's what that looks like:

- **Included:** Employees feel integral to the team's success. *("Keep them in the loop!")*
- **Valued:** Their ideas and efforts are recognized as essential to the organization. *("Actively seek their input!")*
- **Appreciated:** Their contributions are acknowledged and celebrated. *("Make sure they know their work matters!")*

An important and fairly easy way of fostering inclusivity is the intentional use of pronouns. Encouraging employees to include their pronouns in email signatures, virtual meeting names, and internal directories normalizes the practice and supports transgender and nonbinary employees. Managers should lead by example, consistently using correct pronouns in all communications. Misusing or neglecting pronouns can create feelings of exclusion and erode psychological safety, while respectful use fosters trust and belonging.

Effective managers don't guess what employees need—they ask. Regular one-on-one check-ins and team meetings provide opportunities for feedback and open dialogue. Acting on this feedback builds trust, respect, and engagement over time.

## Clear Communication and Overcoming Proximity Bias

Clear communication is the foundation of inclusion. Managers should leverage multiple channels—team meetings, weekly email updates, and collaboration tools like Slack—to ensure all employees, regardless of location, have equal access to critical information. The days of relying on impromptu office conversations are over. Leaders must actively work to counteract proximity bias, the unconscious tendency to favor employees who are physically closer over those working remotely.

## Key Points to Consider:

- **Train Managers:** Equip managers with the skills to effectively lead and engage remote employees.
- **Normalize Pronoun Usage:** Encourage all employees to include pronouns in email signatures and virtual meeting platforms. Educate managers on the importance of using correct pronouns to support an inclusive workplace.
- **Establish Team "Office Hours":** Create informal drop-in sessions where employees can discuss topics without scheduling formal

meetings. Rotate leadership for these sessions to encourage broader participation.

- **Set Virtual Meeting Expectations:** Establish clear guidelines for virtual meetings, including when cameras should be on to promote engagement.
- **Involve Virtual Team Members:** Include virtual team members in planning events to ensure diverse perspectives are considered.
- **Host Virtual Team-Building Activities:** Strengthen connections between remote and in-office employees through interactive activities.
- **Enhance Hybrid Meeting Experiences:** For in-person meetings streamed to remote participants, design interactive elements to ensure virtual attendees feel equally involved.

By intentionally fostering a culture that supports remote and hybrid work while affirming individual identities, organizations can create more inclusive environments, strengthen team cohesion, and inspire employees to perform at their best—regardless of where they work.

# Actionable Strategy 9

Actionable Strategy #9:

Adopt Flexible Work Arrangements:

A Key to Engagement

It's important to distinguish between flexible work arrangements and work accommodations. A work accommodation is a legal obligation of employers in response to reasonable requests of an individual employee, often for a temporary period. In contrast, flexible work arrangements are standard business practices designed to benefit the broader workforce, aligning employee well-being with organizational goals.

Flexible work arrangements are not a novel concept. Options such as flexible hours, compressed workweeks (e.g., four-day workweeks), and part-time schedules have existed for years. However, these benefits have traditionally been reserved for senior executives. For instance, it's common for senior leaders to commute across the country, work four days a week, and spend weekends at home or balance part-time schedules with other business interests.

Yet, what about employees with long commutes due to housing affordability challenges? Allowing them to adjust their work hours to avoid peak traffic could significantly enhance their productivity and morale. This simple adjustment demonstrates how flexibility benefits both the individual and the organization.

## The Essential Question for Leaders

The key question for leaders is: *How can we create a win-win solution for both the business and our employees?* Do all employees need to adhere to a rigid 9-to-5 schedule, or can work be structured around essential tasks and collaboration that require synchronous efforts? With advancements in technology, many tasks can be completed remotely, at any time, and from any location—rendering traditional schedules increasingly outdated.

## Flexibility in a Diverse Workforce

Today's workforce is multigenerational and diverse, encompassing employees with varying responsibilities and abilities. This includes caregivers of children or elderly relatives, individuals balancing personal and professional commitments, and neurodivergent employees who may perform best during non-traditional hours. Additionally, caregiving roles are no longer confined to women; men are increasingly stepping into these roles during standard business hours.

Recognizing these realities and offering flexible work options is not only compassionate but also a smart business strategy. Flexible work arrangements foster engagement, reduce burnout, and improve retention—ultimately benefiting both employees and the organization.

## Key Points to Consider:

- **Flexible Schedules**: Allow employees to start and end their workdays earlier or later to fit their personal needs.
- **Part-Time Options**: Provide part-time schedules with proportionate compensation.
- **Compressed Workweeks**: Implement a 40-hour workweek spread across four days instead of five.
- **Floating Holidays**: Offer paid "floating holidays" to give employees flexibility for personal matters.
- **Job-Sharing Arrangements**: Explore job-sharing options to maintain continuity while supporting flexibility.

While some roles require strict on-site attendance or adherence to set hours, creative solutions can introduce flexibility even within those constraints. The focus should remain on meeting business goals while ensuring employees feel supported and valued.

# Reflection Questions

- What steps can you take to make remote work more inclusive for your team?
- How can you implement flexible work arrangements in your organization?
- What virtual team-building activities can enhance team cohesion?
- What changes can you implement in the next 30, 60, or 90 days to ensure employees feel included, valued, and appreciated?

As companies continue to adapt to remote and hybrid work models, the importance of employee wellness and resilience has never been greater. In the next chapter, we'll explore how integrating DE&I principles with mental health initiatives can prioritize employee well-being and drive sustainable success.

# Chapter 5:
# Fostering Employee Well-being and Resilience

> *"Take care of your employees, and they'll take care of your business."*
>
> *— **Richard Branson***

As a society, there has been a significant push to normalize mental health discussions and address related issues openly. This cultural shift has placed employee wellness at the forefront of workplace priorities. Corporate leaders increasingly recognize that what happens outside the office impacts how employees show up for work—and that what happens at work, in turn, affects life at home. This is especially true for employees who work remotely, where the boundaries between personal and professional lives often blur. Acknowledging that employees cannot, and should not, be expected to separate their personal and professional lives with the flip of a switch is foundational to fostering an inclusive workplace culture.

Merriam-Webster defines **personhood** as "the state of being a person or having human characteristics and feelings." This definition prompts a critical question for leaders who aim to sustain profitability, achieve market growth, and maintain a competitive edge: Do we sometimes lose sight of the humanity of the people who help us achieve these goals?

Losing focus on the human element in business is often unintentional. However, when the drive for organizational success overshadows a leader's ability to recognize the personhood—the humanity—of their employees, the organization ultimately suffers.

Consider the real and deeply troubling case of a 60-year-old female employee found deceased in her office four days after entering the building of a global banking institution in Tempe, Arizona. The fact that her absence went unnoticed for days is a stark and egregious reminder of what can happen when an organization loses sight of the humanity of its employees.

When employees feel their humanity is not prioritized, companies risk losing talented individuals who no longer feel valued. This extends beyond mere respect; it is about being treated with dignity and being recognized for who they are—not just for what they can produce. Leaders who prioritize and nurture the personhood of their employees will be better equipped to succeed in the evolving future of work.

Employers who are prepared for this future are exploring innovative wellness initiatives that support employees holistically. These efforts go beyond performance metrics to ensure employees feel cared for, respected, and seen as whole individuals. Employee well-being isn't just a compassionate approach; it's a business imperative for building resilient, high-performing workplace cultures that thrive in the future of work.

# Actionable Strategy 10

# Actionable Strategy #10:
# Link Mental Health and DE&I for Holistic Support

Supporting employees' mental health is essential for building an inclusive and thriving workplace. Companies must go beyond standard Employee Assistance Programs (EAPs), which are often introduced during open enrollment and rarely mentioned afterward. Instead, mental health and wellness should be ongoing priorities woven into the workplace culture.

Managers play a critical role in fostering this environment. They should be trained to recognize signs of mental health concerns and guide employees to appropriate resources—not as mental health professionals, but as informed leaders who can direct their teams to the right support. Healthcare professionals can provide training to help managers identify when an employee may be in distress and how to respond appropriately. Managers themselves should also have access to communication channels for seeking support if needed. Inclusive leadership requires the ability to manage and support individuals with diverse identities and mental health needs.

Traditional EAPs often suffer from low utilization rates due to limited outreach and insufficient options for long-term care. To improve effectiveness, companies should reimagine their mental health offerings, adopting a holistic approach that addresses employees' overall well-being. This could include initiatives like group bereavement support for employees coping with the loss of a colleague.

Beyond providing a limited number of free counseling sessions, organizations should ensure continuity of care by offering affordable, long-term support. This approach prevents employees from being left without viable care pathways once initial sessions are exhausted.

In times of political or social unrest, or following acts of violence or oppression, companies can further demonstrate their commitment to employee well-being by offering mental health days or flexible work arrangements. These measures acknowledge the external stressors impacting employees' mental and emotional health, showing genuine care and support.

Comprehensive mental health programs can also include initiatives like stress management workshops, financial literacy sessions, leadership coaching, and bereavement support. These programs not only enhance employee engagement and productivity but also foster loyalty and strengthen organizational success. Supporting employees' well-being is more than a compassionate gesture—it's a strategic investment in your company's future.

## Key Points to Consider:

- **Foster Work-Life Balance**: Develop policies that enable employees to better balance work and personal commitments, promoting long-term engagement and productivity.
- **Normalize Mental Health PTO**: Encourage senior leaders to openly discuss using Paid Time Off (PTO) for mental health needs and lead by example to help reduce stigma.
- **Reimagine EAPs**: Expand your EAP program to cater to a wide range of life events (e.g., grief counseling, financial planning, budgeting, legal services, and professional coaching) and provide reasonably priced continuity of care beyond free services.

- **Encourage Group Activities**: Organize health-related group activities (e.g., walking groups or workout classes) that foster an inclusive culture and adapt them for remote employees.

By embedding mental health into your DE&I strategy, you create a workplace where employees feel supported, valued, and empowered to succeed—both personally and professionally.

# Actionable Strategy 11

# Actionable Strategy #11: Cultivate a Culture of Psychological Safety to Drive Innovation

Psychological safety is widely discussed, but do we truly understand what it looks like in practice? At its core, psychological safety is an environment where individuals feel secure expressing themselves, sharing ideas, raising concerns, and taking risks without fear of retribution, ridicule, or embarrassment. Leaders who cultivate such environments recognize that these conditions enable employees to unleash their full potential and drive innovation.

In a psychologically safe workplace, employees are empowered to raise objections, challenge the status quo, and question entrenched practices like, "This is how we've always done it." They feel free to make mistakes, knowing that those mistakes are opportunities for growth and learning. Organizations that embrace this mindset often adopt the philosophy of "fail forward fast," encouraging calculated risks as a means to foster creativity and progress.

However, achieving psychological safety requires more than encouraging bold ideas or fostering innovation. It also means addressing behaviors that undermine inclusivity, such as microaggressions—subtle, often unintentional comments or actions that marginalize individuals based on their identity. Left unchecked, microaggressions erode trust, create feelings of exclusion, and compromise an otherwise psychologically safe environment.

## Trust is the Cornerstone of Psychological Safety

Employees in these environments trust their leaders to stand by their word. They believe there will be no retaliation for speaking up or taking thoughtful risks. Equally important, employees trust that when they raise issues—whether about workplace practices, innovation, or incidents like microaggressions—leaders will investigate and take meaningful action. This trust hinges on leadership's commitment to maintaining these standards and fostering a culture that supports both innovation and accountability.

## Addressing Microaggressions and Building Bystander Practices

Microaggressions are insidious in their impact. Examples include dismissive comments like, "You're so articulate" to a Black colleague, or assuming a female employee will take notes in a meeting. These actions may seem trivial but accumulate over time, creating a culture of exclusion and disengagement.

To counteract this, leaders must educate themselves and their teams about the impact of microaggressions and empower employees to act as allies through upstander practices. Upstander practices involve encouraging employees to speak up when they witness inappropriate behavior or subtle exclusions, creating a collective responsibility for fostering inclusivity.

- **Example of Upstander Action:** If a team member interrupts or talks over another employee, a upstander can interject by saying, "I'd like to hear them finish their thought."
- **Leadership Action:** Train employees to recognize microaggressions and equip them with language and strategies to address them in a constructive, non-confrontational manner.

## Building Psychological Safety Requires Intentional Leadership

Psychological safety doesn't develop by accident; it requires deliberate and sustained effort. Like many cultural shifts, the foundation of psychological safety is built through leadership. Leaders set the tone and model the behavior they want to see in their teams.

- **Encourage Contrarian Thinking:** Leaders should praise employees who present contrarian viewpoints, especially when those ideas prompt the team to explore new perspectives and challenge assumptions.
- **Address Negative Behavior Immediately:** Judgment, ridicule, or microaggressions directed at employees must be addressed promptly. Allowing such behavior to go unchecked erodes trust and stifles open dialogue.
- **Acknowledge Mistakes Transparently:** Leaders should publicly acknowledge their own mistakes, reinforcing the idea that the workplace is a safe space for growth—as long as lessons are learned and adjustments are made. This vulnerability builds trust and resilience within the team.

## The Leadership Imperative

Leaders play a critical role in embedding psychological safety into an organization's culture. This goes beyond merely tolerating differing viewpoints; it requires actively creating opportunities for all voices to be heard and ensuring every employee feels valued and included. Leaders must demonstrate that dissent and innovation are welcomed equally, and that mistakes or incidents of harm, like microaggressions, are addressed with integrity and accountability.

## A Culture That Thrives

By fostering psychological safety, organizations create an environment where employees feel empowered to contribute their ideas, take risks, and challenge the norm. This culture not only drives innovation but also builds trust and engagement, ensuring that employees feel valued and supported as integral members of the team.

## Key Points to Consider:

- **Establish Guidelines:** Develop meeting protocols that encourage employees to voice differing opinions and create a framework for conducting healthy, respectful debates when disagreements arise.
- **Address Microaggressions:** Provide training to help employees recognize and address microaggressions in real-time, fostering a culture of awareness and accountability.
- **Promote Upstander Practices:** Empower employees to intervene constructively when witnessing exclusionary behavior, ensuring collective responsibility for inclusivity.
- **Involve All Voices:** Send meeting agendas in advance and intentionally include diverse perspectives, avoiding reliance on the same familiar contributors.
- **Praise Risk-Taking:** Acknowledge team members who share unconventional ideas, even if those ideas aren't widely accepted, to reinforce a culture of trust and openness.

By integrating psychological safety, addressing microaggressions, and promoting upstander practices, organizations can create a workplace culture that prioritizes trust, fosters innovation, and supports employees in achieving their full potential.

# Actionable Strategy 12

# Actionable Strategy #12:
# Engage Employees Through Listening Sessions

In sales, many corporate leaders pride themselves on listening to the Voice of the Customer (VOC). Yet, in my experience, leaders often fail to place equal importance on the Voice of the Employee (VOE)—missing an opportunity to truly understand their employees' lived experiences within and beyond the workplace.

Effective communication between leaders and employees is critical to fostering an inclusive culture. While surveys and feedback tools are common, listening sessions offer something unique: direct, open dialogue about matters that employees find important. These sessions not only provide insights into the employee experience but also foster trust and engagement.

Poor communication in the workplace carries significant consequences. A survey of 400 companies with 100,000 employees each cited an average loss per company of $62.4 million per year due to inadequate communication to and between employees.[7] This staggering figure underscores the need for leaders to actively prioritize communication as part of their organizational strategy, and listening sessions are a vital tool to bridge these costly gaps.

## The Value of Listening Sessions

Listening sessions provide leaders with a dedicated forum to hear employees' concerns on specific issues. These sessions can be guided by company leaders or facilitated by skilled external professionals,

---

[7] Susie Silver, "Navigating Courageous Conversations About Diversity, Equity and Inclusion," *Training Industry*, August 29, 2022, https://trainingindustry.com/articles/diversity-equity-and-inclusion/navigating-courageous-conversations-about-diversity-equity-and-inclusion/.

creating a supportive and open environment. If conducted internally, leaders must be trained to handle challenging conversations in ways that encourage resolution and healing. Engaging external facilitators can offer additional benefits, such as impartiality and expertise in guiding complex discussions. External facilitators bring an unbiased perspective, helping employees feel safe to share without fear of judgment or retaliation.

In my own experience facilitating such sessions, I've witnessed their transformative potential—especially when leaders show genuine interest and a willingness to act. Asking thoughtful, curious questions can uncover root causes of issues, paving the way for meaningful solutions. Listening sessions not only highlight areas for improvement but also reinforce leadership's commitment to fostering an inclusive and supportive workplace culture.

## Psychological Safety Enables Participation

Psychological safety is a prerequisite for successful listening sessions. Employees must trust that their feedback will be taken seriously and acted upon; and that there will be no retaliation for what's shared. Without this trust, employees are unlikely to engage fully, and the sessions will lose their value. The true measure of success lies not just in listening but in taking meaningful action based on employee input.

## Key Points to Consider:

- **Schedule Regular Listening Sessions:** Host monthly sessions at the department level and quarterly at the divisional or company-wide level (for smaller organizations).
- **Invest in External Facilitators:** External facilitators bring objectivity and expertise, helping transform feedback into actionable tips that enhance workplace culture.
- **Follow Up on Feedback:** Address issues raised during sessions with transparency. Whether through an email update or follow-up discussions, ensure employees know their concerns are being addressed.

# Reflection Questions

- How have you advocated for employees to prioritize their well-being?
- Recall a time when you felt psychologically unsafe at work. What can you learn from that experience to improve workplace culture for your employees?
- What actionable steps can you take in the next 30, 60, or 90 days to foster inclusivity and engagement?

Creating an inclusive workplace culture requires leaders to center their efforts on the needs of employees. In the next chapter, we'll explore how leaders can navigate controversial topics while aligning organizational actions with company values and strengthening trust with both employees and customers.

# Chapter 6:
# Navigating DE&I Challenges in Today's Polarized Climate

> *We can disagree and still love each other unless your disagreement is rooted in my oppression and denial of my humanity and right to exist."*
>
> ***– James Baldwin***

The debate about whether corporate leaders should address controversial or contentious topics is both timely and complex. Should companies take a public stance on policy issues and risk being seen as activist organizations, or remain silent and focus solely on their operations? While some argue that corporations should stay out of social issues, others believe their input and influence are crucial in shaping a better society.

Deciding whether and how to engage with hot-button topics is far from straightforward. It's neither practical nor wise for companies to address every social or political issue that emerges. Yet, the decision to engage isn't always black and white; it often resides in the gray area, where nuanced judgment is required.

## The Impact of External Issues on the Workplace

What happens outside the office—whether it's a national political movement, a global crisis, or local community unrest—doesn't stay outside. These external forces shape how employees feel, how they show up to work, and how they perform their roles. Ignoring this reality is not a viable option for organizations committed to fostering an inclusive and supportive workplace.

Forward-thinking leaders understand that, at a minimum, they must acknowledge the issues that directly impact their employees. Doing so demonstrates empathy and creates an environment where employees feel seen and supported. However, acknowledging an issue doesn't necessarily mean taking a public stance. Leaders must evaluate the context, potential consequences, and alignment with the company's core values before making a decision.

## Balancing Responsibility with Pragmatism

Engaging with contentious topics requires a balance between responsibility and pragmatism. Leaders must consider the following:

- **Alignment with Core Values**: Does the issue align with the company's stated values and purpose? Addressing topics that are consistent with your organization's principles will strengthen trust and authenticity.
- **Impact on Stakeholders**: How does the issue affect your employees, customers, and broader community? Prioritizing issues that have a direct impact on these groups will ensure your response is relevant and meaningful.
- **Relevance to Business Goals**: Does engaging with this issue support or hinder your strategic objectives? Leaders must weigh the benefits of engagement against the risks to their operations, brand reputation, and employee morale.

## Acknowledging, Not Always Acting

It's important to note that acknowledgment doesn't always mean action. Sometimes, listening and providing support internally is more impactful than making a public declaration. For example, if a national event causes widespread emotional distress among employees, creating space for dialogue and offering mental health resources can be more effective than issuing a public statement.

## Leading with Empathy and Strategy

The role of leadership in navigating these challenges cannot be overstated. Empathy must guide the decision-making process, but it should be paired with strategic thinking. Leaders must ask themselves:

- **What do our employees need right now to feel supported and valued?**
- **How can we align our response with our organizational mission and values?**
- **What are the potential short- and long-term implications of speaking out—or staying silent?**

By addressing these questions thoughtfully, leaders can make informed decisions that prioritize both employee well-being and organizational sustainability.

## The Path Forward

Navigating today's complex social and political landscape requires courage, intentionality, and a deep commitment to inclusion. While it's impossible to satisfy everyone, leaders who remain grounded in their values, empathetic to their employees, and strategic in their actions will be better equipped to foster trust, resilience, and a sense of belonging in their organizations.

In the next section, we'll delve deeper into strategies for addressing contentious topics while maintaining alignment with company goals and building a stronger connection with your workforce.

# Actionable Strategy 13

# Actionable Strategy #13:
# Resist Anti-DE&I Pressure

In the wake of the social unrest during the summer of 2020, sparked by the unjustified police killings of Breonna Taylor, an unarmed Black woman, and George Floyd, an unarmed Black man, many companies made public commitments to advancing DE&I. These commitments led to hiring DE&I practitioners, hosting unconscious bias training sessions, establishing dedicated departments, setting quotas for diverse representation, and launching programs aimed at supporting marginalized groups. Often, these initiatives were driven by a desire to meet external benchmarks, such as those set by the Human Rights Campaign or "Best Place to Work" designations.

However, just a few years later, many organizations are retreating from these promises. The lack of a sincere internalization of the injustices highlighted during this time—and how they manifest within corporate spaces—has led to a significant backpedaling. Companies are withdrawing their support for advancing diversity, equity, and inclusion.

## Stay the Course

Organizations genuinely committed to fostering inclusive and equitable workplace cultures remain steadfast in the face of opposition. These companies ensure their DE&I strategies align with core company values and strategic business goals, embedding DE&I into their organizational identity.

Every business decision involves a level of risk, and integrating DE&I as a core strategy is no exception. Resistance may come from individuals or groups who prefer maintaining the status quo, where systemic bias and inequities persist. Claims of reverse discrimination or potential legal challenges may arise. However, by applying the strategies outlined in this book, particularly those in Chapter 1, organizations can build the resilience needed to withstand anti-DE&I pressure.

## The Risks of Retreat

Succumbing to anti-DE&I sentiment without an alternative plan to support employees who feel excluded or overlooked can have significant consequences. Productivity may decline, innovation can stagnate, and retention rates may plummet. Employees who feel undervalued or unsupported are less likely to contribute meaningfully to their organizations, and companies that fail to act risk falling behind in the competitive market.

## Build a Resilient Workplace

Strategic DE&I programming prioritizes equity and inclusivity, helping organizations create a resilient workplace culture. Companies that integrate DE&I strategies into the fabric of their business will reap long-term benefits that transcend the temporary noise of today's political climate.

## Key Points to Consider:

- **Leverage Employee Data**: Use employee feedback and demographic data to justify and support DE&I interventions.
- **Ensure Inclusivity**: Design DE&I programs that benefit all employees rather than focusing exclusively on one group.
- **Align External Partnerships**: Partner with organizations and programs that reflect your company's core values.

- **Guarantee Legal Compliance**: Work closely with your legal team to ensure all DE&I efforts comply with applicable laws.

Resisting anti-DE&I pressure is not just about maintaining a commitment to diversity; it's about fostering an environment where all employees feel valued, supported, and empowered to succeed. Leaders who stay the course will build organizations that thrive—today and in the future.

# Actionable Strategy 14

# Actionable Strategy #14:
# Reject Institutional Neutrality

Anti-DE&I advocates, often under the guise of rejecting so-called "woke" policies, are pressuring companies to "stay in their lane" by embracing institutional neutrality. This concept, originally rooted in academia, has permeated corporate workplaces. It reflects the belief that companies should avoid involvement in societal and political issues, focusing solely on their core business functions—producing, marketing, and selling products. Proponents of institutional neutrality argue that businesses should not acknowledge, advocate, or speak on matters impacting employees or the communities where they operate.

These advocates essentially call for corporate leaders to turn a blind eye to the realities of their workplaces, local communities, and the broader world. However, this approach ignores the interconnected nature of businesses and the communities they serve.

## The Flaws of Institutional Neutrality

Organizations do not exist in isolation. Their operations influence both employees and the communities in which they are embedded. A company's presence—through offices, warehouses, or local initiatives—has tangible effects on the people within those spaces. Anti-DE&I proponents push for companies to overlook this impact, but businesses are inherently part of society. Employees live and work in these communities, and a company's actions, or lack thereof, shape not only internal culture but also external perceptions.

Institutional neutrality often does more harm than good. Employees increasingly want to align with organizations whose values reflect their own. When injustices or harm affect marginalized groups, silence or apathy from leadership sends a harmful message: that the struggles of these communities—and by extension, the employees who identify with or care about those groups—are not valued.

## Taking a Stand

Leaders must regularly assess how their company's purpose, core values, and DE&I goals intersect with broader social issues. This alignment can provide a decision-making framework for determining when and how to engage with societal challenges. Consistency in applying this framework is crucial. Advocating for one group's rights while ignoring the injustices faced by another can erode trust and undermine credibility.

Inconsistencies between internal DE&I initiatives and external actions often lead employees to question leadership's commitment to inclusion, resulting in disengagement and diminished morale. Employees expect more than performative statements; they want action that reflects the company's stated values.

By rejecting institutional neutrality and taking meaningful stands on societal issues aligned with core values, companies can reduce the risk of "optical inclusivity"—performative actions that lack genuine substance.

## Key Points to Consider:

- **Consult Employee Resource Groups (ERGs):** When a societal issue impacts a marginalized group, consult ERG leadership to understand the collective experiences of the group. Ask what support they need from the organization and strive to provide it.

- **Prioritize Humanity**: DE&I work is fundamentally about people. If you're unsure what to say about an issue, start with empathy. Reflect on how the issue may affect your employees. Put yourself in their shoes and ask, "What would I need?" Then, engage directly with affected groups to determine how the organization can provide meaningful support.
- **Recognize Brand Impact:** Institutional neutrality not only negatively affects employees but can also harm your brand, as consumers increasingly expect companies to take a stand on issues that matter.

Rejecting institutional neutrality is not about weighing in on every issue—it's about taking intentional, values-driven actions that align with your organization's purpose and prioritize the humanity of your employees. By doing so, leaders can build trust, strengthen employee engagement, and position their organizations as authentically inclusive workplaces.

# Actionable Strategy 15

# Actionable Strategy #15:
# Champion Equity

To fully engage with this section, we need a shared understanding of equity. Too often, leaders use equity and equality interchangeably, but these terms are fundamentally different.

Equality means giving everyone the same resources or opportunities, assuming that everyone starts from the same place. Equity, however, acknowledges that individuals begin at different starting points due to systemic and structural disparities. Where equality falls short, equity bridges the gap by offering people what they specifically need to thrive, grounded in principles of fairness and justice.

Equity-focused actions aim to level the playing field for those of marginalized identities, ensuring they have a fair chance at success. However, many corporate practices and systems perpetuate longstanding disparities rooted in societal norms. These inequities—originally designed to exclude certain groups—persist today, manifesting as both disparate treatment and disparate impact on people of color and other marginalized communities. For example, parental leave policies often fail to support same-sex couples or don't grant non-birthing parents equal bonding time as birthing parents, reinforcing inequities in caregiving responsibilities.

A crucial part of embracing equity is recognizing how privilege operates alongside systemic barriers. Privilege, often masked as "merit," frequently eases the path for members of dominant groups—typically white, male, cisgender, and able-bodied individuals—even if they are unaware of it. Some leaders resist acknowledging privilege, believing their successes are solely the result of hard work. This perspective overlooks the reality that they may not have faced the same systemic hurdles as their peers from marginalized communities. Additionally, they may have received the benefit of the doubt in situations where others were unfairly judged or excluded. Recognizing privilege is not about diminishing personal effort; it's about understanding the broader systems that create unequal access to opportunities.

Whether this resistance to acknowledging inequities is intentional or unconscious, the outcome is the same: unequal access to opportunities. Transparent and honest conversations about systemic inequities are essential for dismantling biases. These discussions aren't about placing blame or fostering guilt; instead, they are about promoting understanding, accountability, and meaningful change.

## Advancing Equity in the Workplace

Leveling the playing field or advancing equity is not about granting special privileges—it's about removing barriers so everyone has a fair chance to succeed. For example, encouraging and supporting male employees to take advantage of flexible work schedules in response to caregiving responsibilities demonstrates a commitment to equity. If women are the only ones expected to utilize these benefits, they could face bias or be penalized in their career progression. Encouraging men to participate in such programs helps normalize caregiving responsibilities for all genders and mitigates inequitable outcomes.

Equity ensures that all individuals, regardless of their starting point, have access to the opportunities they need to thrive. While DE&I work encompasses a range of equity issues, achieving racial equity remains a critical focus. Leaders must actively identify and address biased practices that hinder the hiring, promotion, and advancement of Black, Brown, and other marginalized individuals. Proactive leadership, combined with intentional strategies, is essential for creating equitable pathways to success.

## Key Points to Consider:

- **Conduct an equity audit:** Evaluate your people policies and programs to identify who has benefited from these policies and who may have been excluded.
- **Perform a pay equity audit:** Examine pay discrepancies and challenge business justifications rooted in bias, ensuring they do not continue unchecked.
- **Create inclusive policies:** Ensure benefits and programs, such as parental leave and caregiving support, address the needs of diverse family structures.

By embracing equity, leaders can disrupt entrenched biases and foster a culture where all employees can thrive. This commitment to equity not only improves individual experiences but also strengthens the organization, creating a foundation for sustainable success.

## **Reflection Questions**

- When was the last time you chose the path of institutional or corporate neutrality? Why?
- What impact did that decision have on your employees? Did you seek their input?
- How did the statements in this section about systemic disparities and racial inequities make you feel? Are you experiencing any resistance to those statements? Why?
- What can you do to embrace equity in the next 30, 60, or 90 days?

_____

_____

_____

_____

_____

_____

_____

_____

As we conclude our exploration of how Diversity, Equity, and Inclusion (DE&I) strategies shape the future of work, it's essential to focus on the core theme: values. The future of work isn't just about adapting to new technologies or evolving business models—it's about grounding your organization in a clear sense of purpose, driven by your core values.

In the final chapter, we'll explore how these values can serve as your North Star, guiding your organization through an ever-changing landscape. Now is the time to rethink leadership, success, and the lasting impact your company has on both employees and consumers.

# Conclusion: Leading the Future of Work with Purpose and Values

> *"You don't build a business. You build people, and people build the business."*
>
> **— *Zig Ziglar***

*I*n 1997, Steve Jobs reintroduced Apple's core values through the iconic "Think Different" campaign, reminding the world that people with passion can change it for the better. This was more than just branding; it was a return to Apple's roots and a reaffirmation of the principles that defined the company's essence. For Apple, these values became a North Star, guiding decisions, fostering innovation, and driving its success.

Similarly, your organization's core values are not just words on a website or a mission statement—they reflect the soul of your company. They should serve as a guiding force behind every decision, action, and strategy. When I work with clients, we always begin by evaluating their core values, mission, and vision, because these elements must be the foundation of their leadership approach. If a decision doesn't align with these principles, the path forward becomes clear.

This alignment also extends to your relationship with consumers. Today's discerning customers can quickly differentiate between genuine actions and performative gestures. They are drawn to businesses with a purpose that goes beyond profit—a purpose that resonates with their own values. When your company's actions are authentically aligned with these values, you foster loyalty, trust, and long-term success. You also attract employees who seek not just a paycheck but meaningful work that aligns with their aspirations and principles.

In today's evolving business landscape, innovation and inclusivity are deeply interconnected. Companies that embrace these principles are the ones that will thrive. As we've explored throughout this book, leading the future of work requires challenging outdated practices, thinking differently, and fostering cultures that prioritize equity and inclusion. The workplace norms of the past are fading, and so too are the customers and employees who accepted them.

Modern consumers and employees alike make decisions based on values. Talented and skilled workers have more options than ever before, and they seek organizations that reflect their priorities. The companies poised to lead tomorrow are those that proactively meet the demands of today's workforce, create inclusive environments, and authentically uphold their core values. Don't let your competitors be the ones to align with these evolving expectations before you do.

The future of work is already here, and it is your responsibility as a leader to shape it. Align your values with your business strategy, embed DE&I into the fabric of your organization, and have the courage to embrace changes that drive innovation and equity. The opportunity to redefine your organization's legacy is here—seize it, and lead your team into a more inclusive, equitable, and successful future.

# Case Studies

## Ben & Jerry's—Advancing Equity Through Activism

Ben & Jerry's is celebrated not only for its ice cream but also for its unwavering commitment to social justice and equity. Activism and advocacy are at the core of the company's identity, guiding its practices and shaping its brand reputation. This dedication is reflected in its mission statement:

*We have a progressive, nonpartisan social mission that seeks to meet human needs and eliminate injustices in our local, national, and international communities by integrating these concerns into our day-to-day business activities.* [8]

From promoting sustainable food production to creating economic opportunities for historically excluded groups, Ben & Jerry's demonstrates that profitability and purpose are not mutually exclusive.[9]

## Building Customer Loyalty Through Advocacy

Ben & Jerry's values-driven approach has deepened customer loyalty by aligning its mission with its operations. Customers recognize and support the company's commitment to social justice, strengthening its leadership in the U.S. ice cream market. This alignment not only bolsters its brand identity but also drives meaningful connections with consumers who prioritize purpose-driven purchases.

---

[8] Ben & Jerry's. (n.d.). *Our progressive values.* Retrieved [November 15, 2024], from https://www.benjerry.com/values/our-progressive-values

[9] *Wall Street Journal,* "How Ben & Jerry's Activism Helps Scoop Up Customers," *The Economics Of* series, June 15, 2022, https://www.wsj.com/video/series/the-economics-of/how-ben-jerrys-activism-helps-scoop-up-customers/4A42DC4B-36B0-4063-A8DF-905D35C604D6.

## Sustained Growth Through Purpose

By authentically championing equity and aligning its corporate actions with its mission, Ben & Jerry's has achieved sustained financial success. Its commitment to addressing societal issues has positioned the company as a leader in both purpose-driven advocacy and profitability, demonstrating that advancing equity can be a core driver of business growth.

Ben & Jerry's exemplifies how aligning corporate values with business practices fosters financial success while making a meaningful social impact.

## Clorox Company—Embedding Equity Into Organizational Culture

Clorox has made significant strides in embedding diversity, equity, and inclusion (DE&I) principles into its organizational practices, creating a workplace where employees feel valued and supported. Through intentional efforts, Clorox demonstrates that prioritizing DE&I can enhance employee satisfaction, drive innovation, and bolster market competitiveness.

## Pay Equity Achievements

In fiscal year 2023, Clorox achieved pay equity for nonproduction teammates across gender globally and race and ethnicity in the U.S.[10] This milestone reflects the company's commitment to fostering a fair and equitable workplace where employees are compensated based on their contributions, without systemic disparities. Regular pay equity audits ensure ongoing fairness and demonstrate Clorox's leadership in addressing inequities within the manufacturing sector.

## Inclusive Workplace Culture

Clorox's inclusion index revealed that 76% of its workforce felt included at work in fiscal year 2023, underscoring the company's efforts to create a supportive environment where employees feel valued and respected. This sense of belonging is further reinforced by Clorox's 4 out of 5-star rating for Diversity and Inclusion on Glassdoor, based on 530 anonymous employee reviews. These metrics reflect a workplace culture that prioritizes inclusion, aligning with industry standards while setting an example for its peers.

---

[10] The Clorox Company. (n.d.). *Leadership commitment to our teammates*. Retrieved December 21, 2024, from https://www.thecloroxcompany.com/company/idea/leadership-commitment-to-our-teammates/

## Leadership Development and Talent Pipelines

To ensure a diverse and equitable workforce, Clorox integrates DE&I principles into its leadership development programs. These initiatives focus on creating pathways for underrepresented groups to advance into leadership roles, fostering a pipeline of diverse talent. By equipping future leaders with the tools to succeed, Clorox strengthens its organizational resilience and positions itself for long-term growth.

## Economic Impact of Purpose-Driven Action

Clorox's dedication to DE&I extends beyond internal culture, driving tangible financial benefits. Inclusive workplace practices have contributed to higher employee retention rates, reduced recruitment costs, and increased innovation by tapping into a diversity of thought and experience. These outcomes, in turn, enhance Clorox's market competitiveness, reinforcing the idea that prioritizing equity and inclusion is not only the right thing to do but also a smart business strategy.

Through its commitment to pay equity, fostering inclusion, and developing diverse leadership, Clorox exemplifies how embedding DE&I principles into every aspect of the organization leads to both cultural and financial success. By prioritizing fairness and opportunity, Clorox has positioned itself as a leader in the manufacturing sector, setting a standard for how companies can thrive in the future of work.

# Epilogue

# A Sobering Shift in the Landscape

At the time of this book's publication, a profound and unsettling shift is taking place within the United States. The current President has issued several executive orders that profoundly impact the foundational principles of equity and inclusion in our nation. Among these is the repeal of Executive Order 11246, originally signed by President Lyndon B. Johnson in 1964—one year before the historic Civil Rights Act was enacted.

Executive Order 11246 was groundbreaking, mandating affirmative action to ensure that federal contractors took proactive steps to eliminate discrimination and foster equal opportunities for all Americans, regardless of race, color, religion, sex, or national origin. Its revocation marks a significant step backward, stripping away critical protections that have underpinned workplace equity for decades.

Even more troubling is the issuance of a new executive order banning diversity, equity, and inclusion (DE&I) programs, policies, and practices within the federal government. This sweeping ban not only dismantles initiatives designed to address systemic inequities but also signals to private sector organizations that prioritizing equity and inclusion is no longer a shared national value.

The consequences of these actions extend far beyond political discourse. They send a clear message: efforts to create workplaces where non-White individuals are valued and empowered to succeed are under attack. For corporate leaders, this presents a moral and strategic dilemma. Do we allow the tides of regression to pull us back to the era of segregation? Or do we stand firm in our commitment to building equitable, inclusive, and high-performing cultures?

By 2045, the United States will become a minority-white nation.[11] Generation Z, born between 1996 and 2012, represents the most ethnically and racially diverse population to date.[12] The future of work demands that employers within the US create welcoming environments where workers of diverse identities and abilities are afforded opportunities to thrive and feel like they belong. There's no getting around that!

The principles outlined in this book are not merely theoretical—they are practical, actionable strategies for creating workplaces that thrive in an ever-changing world. Now more than ever, these strategies must serve as a guide for leaders determined to weather this storm and emerge stronger.

Let this epilogue be a call to action for all leaders who recognize the importance of equity, inclusion, and justice in shaping the future of work. The path forward may be fraught with challenges, but it is a path worth pursuing—not just for the benefit of your organization, but for the betterment of society as a whole.

---

[11] Frey, W. H. (2018, March 14). *The US will become 'minority white' in 2045, Census projects: Youthful minorities are the engine of future growth.* Brookings. Retrieved from https://www.brookings.edu/articles/the-us-will-become-minority-white-in-2045-census-projects/

[12] Pew Research Center. (2020, May 14). *On the cusp of adulthood and facing an uncertain future: What we know about Gen Z so far.* Retrieved from https://www.pewresearch.org/social-trends/2020/05/14/on-the-cusp-of-adulthood-and-facing-an-uncertain-future-what-we-know-about-gen-z-so-far/

As we navigate this critical moment in history, let us lead with courage, conviction, and an unwavering commitment to equity.

# About The Author

**Luaskya C. Nonon, Esq.** is a seasoned attorney with over two decades of experience in employment and corporate transactional law. She is the founder and CEO of **Equity Principle Consulting**, where she partners with corporate leaders to mitigate workplace risks, enhance organizational systems, and build people-first workplace cultures.

Through strategic consulting and coaching, Luaskya helps organizations optimize operations, drive measurable growth, and foster inclusive environments that support long-term success. Her work goes beyond traditional DE&I strategies, focusing on aligning workplace practices with business objectives to create high-performing, sustainable cultures.

Luaskya holds a Bachelor's degree in Psychology from New York University and a Juris Doctorate from the University of North Carolina School of Law. She has earned multiple industry-recognized certifications and awards, including Certified Diversity Professional (CDP®), Certified Personal and Executive Coach, Certified Executive Culture Coach, and the Triangle Business Journal 2023 Diversity Leader Award. Her unique blend of legal expertise, strategic insight, and human-centered approach has established her as a trusted advisor to C-suite leaders navigating workplace transformation.

Luaskya is available for consultancy engagements, leadership coaching, keynotes, corporate training, fireside chats, and panel discussions.

**Connect with Luaskya:**

Website: www.EquityPrinciple.com

Booking: www.MeetwithLuaskya.com

LinkedIn: www.linkedin.com/in/Luaskyanonon

www.ingramcontent.com/pod-product-compliance
Lightning Source LLC
Chambersburg PA
CBHW060500030426
42337CB00015B/1661